These **REFLECTIONS** *and* **PLANS** *belong to:*

Started: / /

Completed: / /

Let your ***aspirations*** become your ***inspirations…***

This isn't only a task planner. It's also a gratitude keeper. It's a place to write down everything that fills your heart as well as your daily plans and to-dos. It's where everything that matters to you will meet.

Because when you give space for your head *and* your heart, your whole world aligns.

GRATITUDE *keeper*

Small or big, briefly sweet or deeply felt... Keep anything and everything that you're grateful for here.

My **FAVORITE** *things*

AFFIRMATIONS, QUOTES & THOUGHTS TO KEEP

BOOKS, PODCASTS & SHOWS TO REMEMBER

PLACES TO VISIT & ADVENTURES TO EXPERIENCE

My ideal **MORNING**

What habits, rituals, or activities make you feel best in the morning? Whether it's making the bed before coffee, or doing a few stretches after taking a walk outside, explore your ideal morning here.

TIME	ROUTINE OR ACTIVITY

What I APPRECIATE *about my current* MORNING *routine:*

ONE THING *I absolutely need each morning to begin the day:*

My ideal **EVENING**

What do you need to wind down the day? Do you need calm and quiet or lots of activity to get your last energy out? Take some time to shape and plan your ideal evening here.

TIME	ROUTINE OR ACTIVITY

What I LOVE *about my current* EVENING *routine:*

ONE THING *I absolutely need each evening to wrap up the day:*

PEOPLE *I love, care for & admire*

WHEN I WAS GROWING UP...

RIGHT NOW...

MOMENTS & MEMORIES *that matter to me*

WHEN I WAS GROWING UP...

RIGHT NOW...

MOOD *tracker*

Pick a color, draw a facial expression, or pencil in a symbol for each emotion—then fill in the box with your foremost mood for each day. Reflect, record, and see if you notice any patterns in your days.

	1	2	3	4	5	6	7	8	9	10	11	12	13	14	15
JAN															
FEB															
MAR															
APR															
MAY															
JUN															
JUL															
AUG															
SEP															
OCT															
NOV															
DEC															

- ☐ *Calm, Peaceful, Content*
- ☐ *Happy, Joyful, Cheerful*
- ☐ *Angry, Frustrated, Upset*
- ☐ *Sad, Emotional, Low*
- ☐ *Energetic, Motivated, Excited*
- ☐ *Nervous, Worried, Edgy*
- ☐ *Fatigued, Tired, Unwell*
- ☐ *Hopeful, Positive, Grateful*
- ☐ *Stressed, Overwhelmed, Strained*
- ☐ *Neutral, Even, Good*

16	17	18	19	20	21	22	23	24	25	26	27	28	29	30	31

MINDFULNESS *tool kit*

Keep your attention close at hand—the activities that calm you, the experiences that restore you, the moments you can create to make life rich and full of wonder.

Notice your breath

Take a slow walk in nature

Look at something ordinary very closely

Light a candle and set an intention

POSITIVITY *prompts*

Take a moment when you can to consider the following. Do your answers surprise you? Reflect on these questions, and the feelings they bring, often.

What is a beautiful moment that happens every day?

What is something you're looking forward to?

What about today is better than yesterday?

What are your strengths? How have they helped you?

Who has helped you become the person you are?

If you were to write a thank you letter to your past self, what would you say?

Recurring **TO-DOS**

WEEKLY

MONTHLY

YEARLY

Biggest **DREAMS** *&* **HOPES** *for the year*

TODAY

Date / /   S M T W T F S

NOTES

TODAY'S INTENTION *or affirmation*

WANT-TOS & HAVE-TOS

ONE THING *that happened today that I'm grateful for:*

IDEAS *& inspiration*

NOTES

Date / / S M T W T F S

TODAY

TODAY'S INTENTION *or affirmation*

WANT-TOS & HAVE-TOS

ONE THING *that happened today that I'm grateful for:*

IDEAS *& inspiration*

TODAY

Date / /   S M T W T F S

NOTES

TODAY'S INTENTION *or affirmation*

WANT-TOS & HAVE-TOS

ONE THING *that happened today that I'm grateful for:*

IDEAS *& inspiration*

NOTES

Date / /

S M T W T F S

TODAY

TODAY'S INTENTION *or affirmation*

WANT-TOS & HAVE-TOS

ONE THING *that happened today that I'm grateful for:*

IDEAS *& inspiration*

TODAY

Date / /

S M T W T F S

NOTES

TODAY'S INTENTION *or affirmation*

WANT-TOS & HAVE-TOS

- ○
- ○
- ○
- ○
- ○
- ○
- ○
- ○
- ○
- ○
- ○
- ○
- ○
- ○

ONE THING *that happened today that I'm grateful for:*

IDEAS *& inspiration*

NOTES

Date / /

S M T W T F S

TODAY

TODAY'S INTENTION *or affirmation*

WANT-TOS & HAVE-TOS

ONE THING *that happened today that I'm grateful for:*

IDEAS *& inspiration*

TODAY

Date / /

S M T W T F S

NOTES

TODAY'S INTENTION *or affirmation*

WANT-TOS & HAVE-TOS

ONE THING *that happened today that I'm grateful for:*

IDEAS *& inspiration*

NOTES

Date / /

S M T W T F S

TODAY

TODAY'S INTENTION *or affirmation*

WANT-TOS & HAVE-TOS

ONE THING *that happened today that I'm grateful for:*

IDEAS *& inspiration*

TODAY

Date / /   S M T W T F S

NOTES

TODAY'S INTENTION *or affirmation*

WANT-TOS & HAVE-TOS

ONE THING *that happened today that I'm grateful for:*

IDEAS *& inspiration*

NOTES

Date / / S M T W T F S

TODAY

TODAY'S INTENTION *or affirmation*

WANT-TOS & HAVE-TOS

ONE THING *that happened today that I'm grateful for:*

IDEAS *& inspiration*

TODAY

Date / /

S M T W T F S

NOTES

TODAY'S INTENTION *or affirmation*

WANT-TOS & HAVE-TOS

ONE THING *that happened today that I'm grateful for:*

IDEAS *& inspiration*

NOTES

Date / /

S M T W T F S

TODAY

TODAY'S INTENTION *or affirmation*

WANT-TOS & HAVE-TOS

ONE THING *that happened today that I'm grateful for:*

IDEAS *& inspiration*

TODAY

Date / /   S M T W T F S

NOTES

TODAY'S INTENTION *or affirmation*

WANT-TOS & HAVE-TOS

ONE THING *that happened today that I'm grateful for:*

IDEAS *& inspiration*

NOTES

Date / /

S M T W T F S

TODAY

TODAY'S INTENTION *or affirmation*

WANT-TOS & HAVE-TOS

ONE THING *that happened today that I'm grateful for:*

IDEAS *& inspiration*

TODAY

Date / /

S M T W T F S

NOTES

TODAY'S INTENTION *or affirmation*

WANT-TOS & HAVE-TOS

ONE THING *that happened today that I'm grateful for:*

IDEAS *& inspiration*

NOTES

Date / /

S M T W T F S

TODAY

TODAY'S INTENTION *or affirmation*

WANT-TOS & HAVE-TOS

ONE THING *that happened today that I'm grateful for:*

IDEAS *& inspiration*

TODAY

Date / /   S M T W T F S

NOTES

TODAY'S INTENTION *or affirmation*

WANT-TOS & HAVE-TOS

- ○
- ○
- ○
- ○
- ○
- ○
- ○
- ○
- ○
- ○
- ○
- ○
- ○
- ○

ONE THING *that happened today that I'm grateful for:*

IDEAS *& inspiration*

NOTES

Date / /

S M T W T F S

TODAY

TODAY'S INTENTION *or affirmation*

WANT-TOS & HAVE-TOS

ONE THING *that happened today that I'm grateful for:*

IDEAS *& inspiration*

TODAY

Date / /

S M T W T F S

NOTES

TODAY'S INTENTION *or affirmation*

WANT-TOS & HAVE-TOS

ONE THING *that happened today that I'm grateful for:*

IDEAS *& inspiration*

NOTES

Date / /

S M T W T F S

TODAY

TODAY'S INTENTION *or affirmation*

WANT-TOS & HAVE-TOS

ONE THING *that happened today that I'm grateful for:*

IDEAS *& inspiration*

TODAY

Date / /   S M T W T F S

NOTES

TODAY'S INTENTION *or affirmation*

WANT-TOS & HAVE-TOS

- ○
- ○
- ○
- ○
- ○
- ○
- ○
- ○
- ○
- ○
- ○
- ○
- ○
- ○

ONE THING *that happened today that I'm grateful for:*

IDEAS *& inspiration*

NOTES

Date / /

S M T W T F S

TODAY

TODAY'S INTENTION *or affirmation*

WANT-TOS & HAVE-TOS

ONE THING *that happened today that I'm grateful for:*

IDEAS *& inspiration*

TODAY

Date / /

S M T W T F S

NOTES

TODAY'S INTENTION *or affirmation*

WANT-TOS & HAVE-TOS

ONE THING *that happened today that I'm grateful for:*

IDEAS *& inspiration*

NOTES

Date / /

S M T W T F S

TODAY

TODAY'S INTENTION *or affirmation*

WANT-TOS & HAVE-TOS

ONE THING *that happened today that I'm grateful for:*

IDEAS *& inspiration*

TODAY

Date / /

S M T W T F S

NOTES

TODAY'S INTENTION *or affirmation*

WANT-TOS & HAVE-TOS

- ○
- ○
- ○
- ○
- ○
- ○
- ○
- ○
- ○
- ○
- ○
- ○
- ○
- ○

ONE THING *that happened today that I'm grateful for:*

IDEAS *& inspiration*

NOTES

Date / /

S M T W T F S

TODAY

TODAY'S INTENTION *or affirmation*

WANT-TOS & HAVE-TOS

ONE THING *that happened today that I'm grateful for:*

IDEAS *& inspiration*

TODAY

Date / /   S M T W T F S

NOTES

TODAY'S INTENTION *or affirmation*

WANT-TOS & HAVE-TOS

- [ ]
- [ ]
- [ ]
- [ ]
- [ ]
- [ ]
- [ ]
- [ ]
- [ ]
- [ ]
- [ ]
- [ ]
- [ ]
- [ ]

ONE THING *that happened today that I'm grateful for:*

IDEAS *& inspiration*

NOTES

Date / /

S M T W T F S

TODAY

TODAY'S INTENTION *or affirmation*

WANT-TOS & HAVE-TOS

ONE THING *that happened today that I'm grateful for:*

IDEAS *& inspiration*

TODAY

Date / /

S M T W T F S

NOTES

TODAY'S INTENTION *or affirmation*

WANT-TOS & HAVE-TOS

ONE THING *that happened today that I'm grateful for:*

IDEAS *& inspiration*

NOTES

Date / /

S M T W T F S

TODAY

TODAY'S INTENTION *or affirmation*

WANT-TOS & HAVE-TOS

ONE THING *that happened today that I'm grateful for:*

IDEAS *& inspiration*

TODAY

Date / /   S M T W T F S

NOTES

TODAY'S INTENTION *or affirmation*

WANT-TOS & HAVE-TOS

ONE THING *that happened today that I'm grateful for:*

IDEAS *& inspiration*

NOTES

Date / /

S M T W T F S

TODAY

TODAY'S INTENTION *or affirmation*

WANT-TOS & HAVE-TOS

ONE THING *that happened today that I'm grateful for:*

IDEAS *& inspiration*

TODAY

Date / /

S M T W T F S

NOTES

TODAY'S INTENTION *or affirmation*

WANT-TOS & HAVE-TOS

- ○
- ○
- ○
- ○
- ○
- ○
- ○
- ○
- ○
- ○
- ○
- ○
- ○
- ○

ONE THING *that happened today that I'm grateful for:*

IDEAS *& inspiration*

NOTES

Date / / S M T W T F S

TODAY

TODAY'S INTENTION *or affirmation*

WANT-TOS & HAVE-TOS

ONE THING *that happened today that I'm grateful for:*

IDEAS *& inspiration*

TODAY

Date / /

S M T W T F S

NOTES

TODAY'S INTENTION *or affirmation*

WANT-TOS & HAVE-TOS

ONE THING *that happened today that I'm grateful for:*

IDEAS *& inspiration*

NOTES

Date / /

S M T W T F S

TODAY

TODAY'S INTENTION *or affirmation*

WANT-TOS & HAVE-TOS

ONE THING *that happened today that I'm grateful for:*

IDEAS *& inspiration*

TODAY

Date / /

S M T W T F S

NOTES

TODAY'S INTENTION *or affirmation*

WANT-TOS & HAVE-TOS

ONE THING *that happened today that I'm grateful for:*

IDEAS *& inspiration*

NOTES

Date / /

S M T W T F S

TODAY

TODAY'S INTENTION *or affirmation*

WANT-TOS & HAVE-TOS

ONE THING *that happened today that I'm grateful for:*

IDEAS *& inspiration*

TODAY

Date / /

S M T W T F S

NOTES

TODAY'S INTENTION *or affirmation*

WANT-TOS & HAVE-TOS

ONE THING *that happened today that I'm grateful for:*

IDEAS *& inspiration*

NOTES

Date / /

S M T W T F S

TODAY

TODAY'S INTENTION *or affirmation*

WANT-TOS & HAVE-TOS

ONE THING *that happened today that I'm grateful for:*

IDEAS *& inspiration*

TODAY

Date / /

S M T W T F S

NOTES

TODAY'S INTENTION *or affirmation*

WANT-TOS & HAVE-TOS

ONE THING *that happened today that I'm grateful for:*

IDEAS *& inspiration*

NOTES

Date / /

S M T W T F S

TODAY

TODAY'S INTENTION *or affirmation*

WANT-TOS & HAVE-TOS

ONE THING *that happened today that I'm grateful for:*

IDEAS *& inspiration*

TODAY

Date / /

S M T W T F S

NOTES

TODAY'S INTENTION *or affirmation*

WANT-TOS & HAVE-TOS

ONE THING *that happened today that I'm grateful for:*

IDEAS *& inspiration*

NOTES

Date / /

S M T W T F S

TODAY

TODAY'S INTENTION *or affirmation*

WANT-TOS & HAVE-TOS

ONE THING *that happened today that I'm grateful for:*

IDEAS *& inspiration*

TODAY

Date / / S M T W T F S

NOTES

TODAY'S INTENTION *or affirmation*

WANT-TOS & HAVE-TOS

ONE THING *that happened today that I'm grateful for:*

IDEAS *& inspiration*

NOTES

Date / /

S M T W T F S

TODAY

TODAY'S INTENTION *or affirmation*

WANT-TOS & HAVE-TOS

ONE THING *that happened today that I'm grateful for:*

IDEAS *& inspiration*

TODAY

Date / /

S M T W T F S

NOTES

TODAY'S INTENTION *or affirmation*

WANT-TOS & HAVE-TOS

ONE THING *that happened today that I'm grateful for:*

IDEAS *& inspiration*

NOTES

Date / /

S M T W T F S

TODAY

TODAY'S INTENTION *or affirmation*

WANT-TOS & HAVE-TOS

ONE THING *that happened today that I'm grateful for:*

IDEAS *& inspiration*

TODAY

Date / /

S M T W T F S

NOTES

TODAY'S INTENTION *or affirmation*

WANT-TOS & HAVE-TOS

ONE THING *that happened today that I'm grateful for:*

IDEAS *& inspiration*

NOTES

Date / /

S M T W T F S

TODAY

TODAY'S INTENTION *or affirmation*

WANT-TOS & HAVE-TOS

ONE THING *that happened today that I'm grateful for:*

IDEAS *& inspiration*

TODAY

Date / /

S M T W T F S

NOTES

TODAY'S INTENTION *or affirmation*

WANT-TOS & HAVE-TOS

ONE THING *that happened today that I'm grateful for:*

IDEAS *& inspiration*

NOTES

Date / / S M T W T F S

TODAY

TODAY'S INTENTION *or affirmation*

WANT-TOS & HAVE-TOS

ONE THING *that happened today that I'm grateful for:*

IDEAS *& inspiration*

TODAY

Date / / S M T W T F S

NOTES

TODAY'S INTENTION *or affirmation*

WANT-TOS & HAVE-TOS

ONE THING *that happened today that I'm grateful for:*

IDEAS *& inspiration*

NOTES

Date / /

S M T W T F S

TODAY

TODAY'S INTENTION *or affirmation*

WANT-TOS & HAVE-TOS

ONE THING *that happened today that I'm grateful for:*

IDEAS *& inspiration*

TODAY

Date / /

S M T W T F S

NOTES

TODAY'S INTENTION *or affirmation*

WANT-TOS & HAVE-TOS

ONE THING *that happened today that I'm grateful for:*

IDEAS *& inspiration*

NOTES

Date / /

S M T W T F S

TODAY

TODAY'S INTENTION *or affirmation*

WANT-TOS & HAVE-TOS

ONE THING *that happened today that I'm grateful for:*

IDEAS *& inspiration*

TODAY

Date / /

S M T W T F S

NOTES

TODAY'S INTENTION *or affirmation*

WANT-TOS & HAVE-TOS

ONE THING *that happened today that I'm grateful for:*

IDEAS *& inspiration*

NOTES

Date / /

S M T W T F S

TODAY

TODAY'S INTENTION *or affirmation*

WANT-TOS & HAVE-TOS

ONE THING *that happened today that I'm grateful for:*

IDEAS *& inspiration*

TODAY

Date / /

S M T W T F S

NOTES

TODAY'S INTENTION *or affirmation*

WANT-TOS & HAVE-TOS

ONE THING *that happened today that I'm grateful for:*

IDEAS *& inspiration*

NOTES

Date / /

S M T W T F S

TODAY

TODAY'S INTENTION *or affirmation*

WANT-TOS & HAVE-TOS

ONE THING *that happened today that I'm grateful for:*

IDEAS *& inspiration*

TODAY

Date / /

S M T W T F S

NOTES

TODAY'S INTENTION *or affirmation*

WANT-TOS & HAVE-TOS

ONE THING *that happened today that I'm grateful for:*

IDEAS *& inspiration*

NOTES

Date / /

S M T W T F S

TODAY

TODAY'S INTENTION *or affirmation*

WANT-TOS & HAVE-TOS

ONE THING *that happened today that I'm grateful for:*

IDEAS *& inspiration*

TODAY

Date / / S M T W T F S

NOTES

TODAY'S INTENTION *or affirmation*

WANT-TOS & HAVE-TOS

- [ ]
- [ ]
- [ ]
- [ ]
- [ ]
- [ ]
- [ ]
- [ ]
- [ ]
- [ ]
- [ ]
- [ ]
- [ ]
- [ ]

ONE THING *that happened today that I'm grateful for:*

IDEAS *& inspiration*

NOTES

Date / /

S M T W T F S

TODAY

TODAY'S INTENTION *or affirmation*

WANT-TOS & HAVE-TOS

ONE THING *that happened today that I'm grateful for:*

IDEAS *& inspiration*

TODAY

Date / /

S M T W T F S

NOTES

TODAY'S INTENTION *or affirmation*

WANT-TOS & HAVE-TOS

ONE THING *that happened today that I'm grateful for:*

IDEAS *& inspiration*

NOTES

Date / /

S M T W T F S

TODAY

TODAY'S INTENTION *or affirmation*

WANT-TOS & HAVE-TOS

ONE THING *that happened today that I'm grateful for:*

IDEAS *& inspiration*

TODAY

Date / /   S M T W T F S

NOTES

TODAY'S INTENTION *or affirmation*

WANT-TOS & HAVE-TOS

ONE THING *that happened today that I'm grateful for:*

IDEAS *& inspiration*

NOTES

Date / /

S M T W T F S

TODAY

TODAY'S INTENTION *or affirmation*

WANT-TOS & HAVE-TOS

ONE THING *that happened today that I'm grateful for:*

IDEAS *& inspiration*

TODAY

Date / /   S M T W T F S

NOTES

TODAY'S INTENTION *or affirmation*

WANT-TOS & HAVE-TOS

ONE THING *that happened today that I'm grateful for:*

IDEAS *& inspiration*

NOTES

Date / /

S M T W T F S

TODAY

TODAY'S INTENTION *or affirmation*

WANT-TOS & HAVE-TOS

ONE THING *that happened today that I'm grateful for:*

IDEAS *& inspiration*

TODAY

Date / /

S M T W T F S

NOTES

TODAY'S INTENTION *or affirmation*

WANT-TOS & HAVE-TOS

ONE THING *that happened today that I'm grateful for:*

IDEAS *& inspiration*

NOTES

Date / /

S M T W T F S

TODAY

TODAY'S INTENTION *or affirmation*

WANT-TOS & HAVE-TOS

ONE THING *that happened today that I'm grateful for:*

IDEAS *& inspiration*

TODAY

Date / /

S M T W T F S

NOTES

TODAY'S INTENTION *or affirmation*

WANT-TOS & HAVE-TOS

ONE THING *that happened today that I'm grateful for:*

IDEAS *& inspiration*

NOTES

Date / /

S M T W T F S

TODAY

TODAY'S INTENTION *or affirmation*

WANT-TOS & HAVE-TOS

- [ ]
- [ ]
- [ ]
- [ ]
- [ ]
- [ ]
- [ ]
- [ ]
- [ ]
- [ ]
- [ ]
- [ ]
- [ ]
- [ ]

ONE THING *that happened today that I'm grateful for:*

IDEAS *& inspiration*

TODAY

Date / /   S M T W T F S

NOTES

TODAY'S INTENTION *or affirmation*

WANT-TOS & HAVE-TOS

ONE THING *that happened today that I'm grateful for:*

IDEAS *& inspiration*

NOTES

Date / /

S M T W T F S

TODAY

TODAY'S INTENTION *or affirmation*

WANT-TOS & HAVE-TOS

ONE THING *that happened today that I'm grateful for:*

IDEAS *& inspiration*

TODAY

Date / / S M T W T F S

NOTES

TODAY'S INTENTION *or affirmation*

WANT-TOS & HAVE-TOS

ONE THING *that happened today that I'm grateful for:*

IDEAS *& inspiration*

NOTES

Date / /

S M T W T F S

TODAY

TODAY'S INTENTION *or affirmation*

WANT-TOS & HAVE-TOS

ONE THING *that happened today that I'm grateful for:*

IDEAS *& inspiration*

TODAY

Date / / S M T W T F S

NOTES

TODAY'S INTENTION *or affirmation*

WANT-TOS & HAVE-TOS

ONE THING *that happened today that I'm grateful for:*

IDEAS *& inspiration*

NOTES

Date / /

S M T W T F S

TODAY

TODAY'S INTENTION *or affirmation*

WANT-TOS & HAVE-TOS

ONE THING *that happened today that I'm grateful for:*

IDEAS *& inspiration*

TODAY

Date / /

S M T W T F S

NOTES

TODAY'S INTENTION *or affirmation*

WANT-TOS & HAVE-TOS

ONE THING *that happened today that I'm grateful for:*

IDEAS *& inspiration*

NOTES

Date / /

S M T W T F S

TODAY

TODAY'S INTENTION *or affirmation*

WANT-TOS & HAVE-TOS

ONE THING *that happened today that I'm grateful for:*

IDEAS *& inspiration*

TODAY

Date / / S M T W T F S

NOTES

TODAY'S INTENTION *or affirmation*

WANT-TOS & HAVE-TOS

ONE THING *that happened today that I'm grateful for:*

IDEAS *& inspiration*

NOTES

Date / /

S M T W T F S

TODAY

TODAY'S INTENTION *or affirmation*

WANT-TOS & HAVE-TOS

ONE THING *that happened today that I'm grateful for:*

IDEAS *& inspiration*

TODAY

Date / /　　S M T W T F S

NOTES

TODAY'S INTENTION *or affirmation*

WANT-TOS & HAVE-TOS

ONE THING *that happened today that I'm grateful for:*

IDEAS *& inspiration*

NOTES

Date / /

S M T W T F S

TODAY

TODAY'S INTENTION *or affirmation*

WANT-TOS & HAVE-TOS

ONE THING *that happened today that I'm grateful for:*

IDEAS *& inspiration*

TODAY

Date / /

S M T W T F S

NOTES

TODAY'S INTENTION *or affirmation*

WANT-TOS & HAVE-TOS

ONE THING *that happened today that I'm grateful for:*

IDEAS *& inspiration*

NOTES

Date / / S M T W T F S

TODAY

TODAY'S INTENTION *or affirmation*

WANT-TOS & HAVE-TOS

ONE THING *that happened today that I'm grateful for:*

IDEAS *& inspiration*

TODAY

Date / /

S M T W T F S

NOTES

TODAY'S INTENTION *or affirmation*

WANT-TOS & HAVE-TOS

- ○
- ○
- ○
- ○
- ○
- ○
- ○
- ○
- ○
- ○
- ○
- ○
- ○
- ○

ONE THING *that happened today that I'm grateful for:*

IDEAS *& inspiration*

NOTES

Date / /

S M T W T F S

TODAY

TODAY'S INTENTION *or affirmation*

WANT-TOS & HAVE-TOS

- ○
- ○
- ○
- ○
- ○
- ○
- ○
- ○
- ○
- ○
- ○
- ○
- ○
- ○

ONE THING *that happened today that I'm grateful for:*

IDEAS *& inspiration*

TODAY

Date / / S M T W T F S

NOTES

TODAY'S INTENTION *or affirmation*

WANT-TOS & HAVE-TOS

- ○
- ○
- ○
- ○
- ○
- ○
- ○
- ○
- ○
- ○
- ○
- ○
- ○
- ○

ONE THING *that happened today that I'm grateful for:*

IDEAS *& inspiration*

NOTES

Date / /

S M T W T F S

TODAY

TODAY'S INTENTION *or affirmation*

WANT-TOS & HAVE-TOS

ONE THING *that happened today that I'm grateful for:*

IDEAS *& inspiration*

TODAY

Date / /

S M T W T F S

NOTES

TODAY'S INTENTION *or affirmation*

WANT-TOS & HAVE-TOS

ONE THING *that happened today that I'm grateful for:*

IDEAS *& inspiration*

NOTES

Date / /

S M T W T F S

TODAY

TODAY'S INTENTION *or affirmation*

WANT-TOS & HAVE-TOS

ONE THING *that happened today that I'm grateful for:*

IDEAS *& inspiration*

TODAY

Date / /

S M T W T F S

NOTES

TODAY'S INTENTION *or affirmation*

WANT-TOS & HAVE-TOS

- ○
- ○
- ○
- ○
- ○
- ○
- ○
- ○
- ○
- ○
- ○
- ○
- ○
- ○

ONE THING *that happened today that I'm grateful for:*

IDEAS *& inspiration*

NOTES

Date / /

S M T W T F S

TODAY

TODAY'S INTENTION *or affirmation*

WANT-TOS & HAVE-TOS

ONE THING *that happened today that I'm grateful for:*

IDEAS *& inspiration*

TODAY

Date / / S M T W T F S

NOTES

TODAY'S INTENTION *or affirmation*

WANT-TOS & HAVE-TOS

ONE THING *that happened today that I'm grateful for:*

IDEAS *& inspiration*

NOTES

Date / /

S M T W T F S

TODAY

TODAY'S INTENTION *or affirmation*

WANT-TOS & HAVE-TOS

ONE THING *that happened today that I'm grateful for:*

IDEAS *& inspiration*

TODAY

Date / /

S M T W T F S

NOTES

TODAY'S INTENTION *or affirmation*

WANT-TOS & HAVE-TOS

ONE THING *that happened today that I'm grateful for:*

IDEAS *& inspiration*

NOTES

Date / /

S M T W T F S

TODAY

TODAY'S INTENTION *or affirmation*

WANT-TOS & HAVE-TOS

ONE THING *that happened today that I'm grateful for:*

IDEAS *& inspiration*

TODAY

Date / /   S M T W T F S

NOTES

TODAY'S INTENTION *or affirmation*

WANT-TOS & HAVE-TOS

ONE THING *that happened today that I'm grateful for:*

IDEAS *& inspiration*

NOTES

Date / /

S M T W T F S

TODAY

TODAY'S INTENTION *or affirmation*

WANT-TOS & HAVE-TOS

ONE THING *that happened today that I'm grateful for:*

IDEAS *& inspiration*

TODAY

Date / /

S M T W T F S

NOTES

TODAY'S INTENTION *or affirmation*

WANT-TOS & HAVE-TOS

ONE THING *that happened today that I'm grateful for:*

IDEAS *& inspiration*

NOTES

Date / / S M T W T F S

TODAY

TODAY'S INTENTION *or affirmation*

WANT-TOS & HAVE-TOS

ONE THING *that happened today that I'm grateful for:*

IDEAS *& inspiration*

TODAY

Date / / S M T W T F S

NOTES

TODAY'S INTENTION *or affirmation*

WANT-TOS & HAVE-TOS

ONE THING *that happened today that I'm grateful for:*

IDEAS *& inspiration*

NOTES

Date / /

S M T W T F S

TODAY

TODAY'S INTENTION *or affirmation*

WANT-TOS & HAVE-TOS

- ◯
- ◯
- ◯
- ◯
- ◯
- ◯
- ◯
- ◯
- ◯
- ◯
- ◯
- ◯
- ◯
- ◯

ONE THING *that happened today that I'm grateful for:*

IDEAS *& inspiration*

TODAY

Date / / S M T W T F S

NOTES

TODAY'S INTENTION *or affirmation*

WANT-TOS & HAVE-TOS

ONE THING *that happened today that I'm grateful for:*

IDEAS *& inspiration*

NOTES

Date / /

S M T W T F S

TODAY

TODAY'S INTENTION *or affirmation*

WANT-TOS & HAVE-TOS

ONE THING *that happened today that I'm grateful for:*

IDEAS *& inspiration*

TODAY

Date / /　　S M T W T F S

NOTES

TODAY'S INTENTION *or affirmation*

WANT-TOS & HAVE-TOS

ONE THING *that happened today that I'm grateful for:*

IDEAS *& inspiration*

NOTES

Date / / S M T W T F S

TODAY

TODAY'S INTENTION *or affirmation*

WANT-TOS & HAVE-TOS

ONE THING *that happened today that I'm grateful for:*

IDEAS *& inspiration*

TODAY

Date / / S M T W T F S

NOTES

TODAY'S INTENTION *or affirmation*

WANT-TOS & HAVE-TOS

ONE THING *that happened today that I'm grateful for:*

IDEAS *& inspiration*

NOTES

Date / /

S M T W T F S

TODAY

TODAY'S INTENTION *or affirmation*

WANT-TOS & HAVE-TOS

ONE THING *that happened today that I'm grateful for:*

IDEAS *& inspiration*

TODAY

Date / /   S M T W T F S

NOTES

TODAY'S INTENTION *or affirmation*

WANT-TOS & HAVE-TOS

- ○
- ○
- ○
- ○
- ○
- ○
- ○
- ○
- ○
- ○
- ○
- ○
- ○
- ○

ONE THING *that happened today that I'm grateful for:*

IDEAS *& inspiration*

NOTES

Date / /

S M T W T F S

TODAY

TODAY'S INTENTION *or affirmation*

WANT-TOS & HAVE-TOS

ONE THING *that happened today that I'm grateful for:*

IDEAS *& inspiration*

TODAY

Date / /

S M T W T F S

NOTES

TODAY'S INTENTION *or affirmation*

WANT-TOS & HAVE-TOS

ONE THING *that happened today that I'm grateful for:*

IDEAS *& inspiration*

NOTES

Date / /

S M T W T F S

TODAY

TODAY'S INTENTION *or affirmation*

WANT-TOS & HAVE-TOS

ONE THING *that happened today that I'm grateful for:*

IDEAS *& inspiration*

TODAY

Date / / S M T W T F S

NOTES

TODAY'S INTENTION *or affirmation*

WANT-TOS & HAVE-TOS

ONE THING *that happened today that I'm grateful for:*

IDEAS *& inspiration*

NOTES

Date / /

S M T W T F S

TODAY

TODAY'S INTENTION *or affirmation*

WANT-TOS & HAVE-TOS

ONE THING *that happened today that I'm grateful for:*

IDEAS *& inspiration*

TODAY

Date / /

S M T W T F S

NOTES

TODAY'S INTENTION *or affirmation*

WANT-TOS & HAVE-TOS

ONE THING *that happened today that I'm grateful for:*

IDEAS *& inspiration*

NOTES

Date / /

S M T W T F S

TODAY

TODAY'S INTENTION *or affirmation*

WANT-TOS & HAVE-TOS

ONE THING *that happened today that I'm grateful for:*

IDEAS *& inspiration*

TODAY

Date / /

S M T W T F S

NOTES

TODAY'S INTENTION *or affirmation*

WANT-TOS & HAVE-TOS

ONE THING *that happened today that I'm grateful for:*

IDEAS *& inspiration*

NOTES

Date / /

S M T W T F S

TODAY

TODAY'S INTENTION *or affirmation*

WANT-TOS & HAVE-TOS

ONE THING *that happened today that I'm grateful for:*

IDEAS *& inspiration*

TODAY

Date / /

S M T W T F S

NOTES

TODAY'S INTENTION *or affirmation*

WANT-TOS & HAVE-TOS

ONE THING *that happened today that I'm grateful for:*

IDEAS *& inspiration*

NOTES

Date / / S M T W T F S

TODAY

TODAY'S INTENTION *or affirmation*

WANT-TOS & HAVE-TOS

ONE THING *that happened today that I'm grateful for:*

IDEAS *& inspiration*

TODAY

Date / /   S M T W T F S

NOTES

TODAY'S INTENTION *or affirmation*

WANT-TOS & HAVE-TOS

ONE THING *that happened today that I'm grateful for:*

IDEAS *& inspiration*

NOTES

Date / /

S M T W T F S

TODAY

TODAY'S INTENTION *or affirmation*

WANT-TOS & HAVE-TOS

ONE THING *that happened today that I'm grateful for:*

IDEAS *& inspiration*

TODAY

Date / /

S M T W T F S

NOTES

TODAY'S INTENTION *or affirmation*

WANT-TOS & HAVE-TOS

- ○
- ○
- ○
- ○
- ○
- ○
- ○
- ○
- ○
- ○
- ○
- ○
- ○
- ○

ONE THING *that happened today that I'm grateful for:*

IDEAS *& inspiration*

NOTES

Date / /

S M T W T F S

TODAY

TODAY'S INTENTION *or affirmation*

WANT-TOS & HAVE-TOS

ONE THING *that happened today that I'm grateful for:*

IDEAS *& inspiration*

TODAY

Date / /   S M T W T F S

NOTES

TODAY'S INTENTION *or affirmation*

WANT-TOS & HAVE-TOS

ONE THING *that happened today that I'm grateful for:*

IDEAS *& inspiration*

NOTES

Date / / S M T W T F S

TODAY

TODAY'S INTENTION *or affirmation*

WANT-TOS & HAVE-TOS

ONE THING *that happened today that I'm grateful for:*

IDEAS *& inspiration*

TODAY

Date / /

S M T W T F S

NOTES

TODAY'S INTENTION *or affirmation*

WANT-TOS & HAVE-TOS

ONE THING *that happened today that I'm grateful for:*

IDEAS *& inspiration*

NOTES

Date / /

S M T W T F S

TODAY

TODAY'S INTENTION *or affirmation*

WANT-TOS & HAVE-TOS

ONE THING *that happened today that I'm grateful for:*

IDEAS *& inspiration*

TODAY

Date / /   S M T W T F S

NOTES

TODAY'S INTENTION *or affirmation*

WANT-TOS & HAVE-TOS

ONE THING *that happened today that I'm grateful for:*

IDEAS *& inspiration*

NOTES

Date / /

S M T W T F S

TODAY

TODAY'S INTENTION *or affirmation*

WANT-TOS & HAVE-TOS

ONE THING *that happened today that I'm grateful for:*

IDEAS *& inspiration*

TODAY

Date / /

S M T W T F S

NOTES

TODAY'S INTENTION *or affirmation*

WANT-TOS & HAVE-TOS

ONE THING *that happened today that I'm grateful for:*

IDEAS *& inspiration*

NOTES

Date / /

S M T W T F S

TODAY

TODAY'S INTENTION *or affirmation*

WANT-TOS & HAVE-TOS

ONE THING *that happened today that I'm grateful for:*

IDEAS *& inspiration*

TODAY

Date / / S M T W T F S

NOTES

TODAY'S INTENTION *or affirmation*

WANT-TOS & HAVE-TOS

- [ ]
- [ ]
- [ ]
- [ ]
- [ ]
- [ ]
- [ ]
- [ ]
- [ ]
- [ ]
- [ ]
- [ ]
- [ ]
- [ ]

ONE THING *that happened today that I'm grateful for:*

IDEAS *& inspiration*

NOTES

Date / /

S M T W T F S

TODAY

TODAY'S INTENTION *or affirmation*

WANT-TOS & HAVE-TOS

ONE THING *that happened today that I'm grateful for:*

IDEAS *& inspiration*

TODAY

Date / /   S M T W T F S   NOTES

TODAY'S INTENTION *or affirmation*

WANT-TOS & HAVE-TOS

ONE THING *that happened today that I'm grateful for:*

IDEAS *& inspiration*

NOTES

Date / / S M T W T F S

TODAY

TODAY'S INTENTION *or affirmation*

WANT-TOS & HAVE-TOS

ONE THING *that happened today that I'm grateful for:*

IDEAS *& inspiration*

TODAY

Date / / S M T W T F S

NOTES

TODAY'S INTENTION *or affirmation*

WANT-TOS & HAVE-TOS

ONE THING *that happened today that I'm grateful for:*

IDEAS *& inspiration*

NOTES

Date / /

S M T W T F S

TODAY

TODAY'S INTENTION *or affirmation*

WANT-TOS & HAVE-TOS

ONE THING *that happened today that I'm grateful for:*

IDEAS *& inspiration*

TODAY

Date / /   S M T W T F S

NOTES

TODAY'S INTENTION *or affirmation*

WANT-TOS & HAVE-TOS

ONE THING *that happened today that I'm grateful for:*

IDEAS *& inspiration*

NOTES

Date / /

S M T W T F S

TODAY

TODAY'S INTENTION *or affirmation*

WANT-TOS & HAVE-TOS

ONE THING *that happened today that I'm grateful for:*

IDEAS *& inspiration*

TODAY

Date / /

S M T W T F S

NOTES

TODAY'S INTENTION *or affirmation*

WANT-TOS & HAVE-TOS

ONE THING *that happened today that I'm grateful for:*

IDEAS *& inspiration*

NOTES

Date / /

S M T W T F S

TODAY

TODAY'S INTENTION *or affirmation*

WANT-TOS & HAVE-TOS

ONE THING *that happened today that I'm grateful for:*

IDEAS *& inspiration*

TODAY

Date / /   S M T W T F S

NOTES

TODAY'S INTENTION *or affirmation*

WANT-TOS & HAVE-TOS

ONE THING *that happened today that I'm grateful for:*

IDEAS *& inspiration*

NOTES

Date / / S M T W T F S

TODAY

TODAY'S INTENTION *or affirmation*

WANT-TOS & HAVE-TOS

ONE THING *that happened today that I'm grateful for:*

IDEAS *& inspiration*

TODAY

Date / / S M T W T F S

NOTES

TODAY'S INTENTION *or affirmation*

WANT-TOS & HAVE-TOS

ONE THING *that happened today that I'm grateful for:*

IDEAS *& inspiration*

NOTES

Date / /

S M T W T F S

TODAY

TODAY'S INTENTION *or affirmation*

WANT-TOS & HAVE-TOS

ONE THING *that happened today that I'm grateful for:*

IDEAS *& inspiration*

TODAY

Date / /   S M T W T F S

NOTES

TODAY'S INTENTION *or affirmation*

WANT-TOS & HAVE-TOS

ONE THING *that happened today that I'm grateful for:*

IDEAS *& inspiration*

NOTES

Date / /

S M T W T F S

TODAY

TODAY'S INTENTION *or affirmation*

WANT-TOS & HAVE-TOS

ONE THING *that happened today that I'm grateful for:*

IDEAS *& inspiration*

TODAY

Date / /   S M T W T F S

NOTES

TODAY'S INTENTION *or affirmation*

WANT-TOS & HAVE-TOS

ONE THING *that happened today that I'm grateful for:*

IDEAS *& inspiration*

NOTES

Date / /

S M T W T F S

TODAY

TODAY'S INTENTION *or affirmation*

WANT-TOS & HAVE-TOS

ONE THING *that happened today that I'm grateful for:*

IDEAS *& inspiration*

TODAY

Date / /

S M T W T F S

NOTES

TODAY'S INTENTION *or affirmation*

WANT-TOS & HAVE-TOS

ONE THING *that happened today that I'm grateful for:*

IDEAS *& inspiration*

NOTES

Date / /

S M T W T F S

TODAY

TODAY'S INTENTION *or affirmation*

WANT-TOS & HAVE-TOS

ONE THING *that happened today that I'm grateful for:*

IDEAS *& inspiration*

TODAY

Date / / S M T W T F S

NOTES

TODAY'S INTENTION *or affirmation*

WANT-TOS & HAVE-TOS

ONE THING *that happened today that I'm grateful for:*

IDEAS *& inspiration*

NOTES

Date / /

S M T W T F S

TODAY

TODAY'S INTENTION *or affirmation*

WANT-TOS & HAVE-TOS

- [ ]
- [ ]
- [ ]
- [ ]
- [ ]
- [ ]
- [ ]
- [ ]
- [ ]
- [ ]
- [ ]
- [ ]
- [ ]
- [ ]

ONE THING *that happened today that I'm grateful for:*

IDEAS *& inspiration*

TODAY

Date / /

S M T W T F S

NOTES

TODAY'S INTENTION *or affirmation*

WANT-TOS & HAVE-TOS

ONE THING *that happened today that I'm grateful for:*

IDEAS *& inspiration*

NOTES

Date / / S M T W T F S

TODAY

TODAY'S INTENTION *or affirmation*

WANT-TOS & HAVE-TOS

ONE THING *that happened today that I'm grateful for:*

IDEAS *& inspiration*

IMPORTANT DATES *& celebrations*

JANUARY	FEBRUARY
MAY	JUNE
SEPTEMBER	OCTOBER

MARCH

APRIL

JULY

AUGUST

NOVEMBER

DECEMBER

Passwords & things to **REMEMBER**

NOTES, IDEAS & DAYDREAMS

REFLECTIONS

Looking back on your time with this daily gratitude and task planner, what is something you've discovered about your life? Are there things or people you would like to hold more closely? Are there experiences or activities you'd like to invite more of? And what are you most looking forward to in the days and weeks ahead?

COMPENDIUM
live inspired

An imprint of the Crown Publishing Group
A division of Penguin Random House LLC
1745 Broadway, New York, NY 10019
live-inspired.com | penguinrandomhouse.com

ISBN: 978-1-957891-92-7

Writer: Amelia Riedler
Designer: Justine Edge
Production Manager: Olivia Holmes

1st printing. Manufactured in Malaysia with mineral oil–free inks on FSC®-Mix certified paper.

The authorized representative in the EU for product safety and compliance is Penguin Random House Ireland, Morrison Chambers, 32 Nassau Street, Dublin D02 YH68, Ireland, https://eu-contact.penguin.ie.

Create meaningful moments with gifts that inspire.